EDGE EFFECTS

also by Jan Conn

Red Shoes in the Rain (1984)
The Fabulous Disguise of Ourselves (1986)
South of the Tudo Bem Café (1990)
What Dante Did with Loss (1994)
Beauties on Mad River (2000)
Jaguar Rain (2006)
Botero's Beautiful Horses (2009)

EDGE EFFECTS

JAN CONN

Brick Books

Library and Archives Canada Cataloguing in Publication

Conn, Jan, 1952–
    Edge effects / Jan Conn.

Poems.
ISBN 978-1-926829-77-7

I. Title.

PS8555.O543E34 2012   C811'.54   C2012-903593-9

We acknowledge the Canada Council for the Arts, the Government of Canada through the Canada Book Fund, and the Ontario Arts Council for their support of our publishing program.

The cover image is a photograph of East Greenbush, NY artist Suzanne Hicks' colour palette.

The author photograph is by Stacy Greene (www.stacygreene.com).

Cover design by Cheryl Dipede.

The book is set in Granjon and Interstate.

Design and layout by Alan Siu.

Printed and bound by Sunville Printco Inc.

Brick Books
431 Boler Road, Box 20081
London, Ontario N6K 4G6

www.brickbooks.ca

for Carlo

for Maria Muszynska

I am far and I am an animal and I am just another I-am poem,

a we-see poem, a they-love poem.
—Peter Gizzi

Contents

Lost Traveller

Labyrinth

The Long Migration

The Vagaries of the Universe

Space Is a Temporal Concept

The snails mount the stairs up the left side
    of the temple, followed by treble notes a cappella,
loud as a jazzed-up car with bass rumbling
    our eardrums, while suspended overhead
is a two-ton Aztec calendar or facsimile.
    The velveteen texture of the golf greens
depends on enough herbicides and fertilizer
    to poison all our drinking water forever.
Centre stage, Wide-Eared Clown and Lord Death
    stand back to back, locked in
sardonic debate, while a roulette wheel spins
    the diorama up onto another level of existence,
for which, dear Diana, not even your spectacular
    marble profile at the Met has prepared us. Now,
two archways rub shoulders, a crane lifts
    wheat and barley fields and multiple heirloom varieties
of hydroponic tomatoes. Every object
    shimmers, images etched across ever more luscious
faces and tender lips. Before thoughts were formed
    they were being broadcast from these diamond-shaped mobiles
in a fever of daylight, but delicately, because time, evil in intent,
    is zipping by. They put your left foot in butter and then
your right foot in and, as the vision recedes, the pastry chef
    is crowned and rides off on a float down Fifth.
The arrow says up. We follow doggedly because
    all the water's transported in metal pipes
and aqueducts. Everyone who makes it to the top is rewarded
    with fountains of clean, aerated H_2O. The children are
offered ice cream, free of course, and we gorge on marshmallows,
    gathered around fires that spring up spontaneously
as far as the eye can see. When we begin the long migration
    toward magnetic north, fault lines underfoot,
deep and ragged, the homeless are with us. Absent
    loved ones join us, my father included,

and all the emotional debris of a lifetime hovers overhead,
    flashing and rotating in a vast vertical column,
as eager to befriend us as a lost puppy.

Beneath Dishevelled Stars

"...even noon is just a lighter night."
—David Mitchell

Among volcanoes, the migrants are cloud-bound,
    their breathing laboured.

Many have left the village—fled across the amorphous line of empire,
    vanished into the desert.

Sunlight catches one horse's eye, inflamed and demonic,
    and the beaded mask of a straggler from last night's carnival
who pauses, footsore, post-euphoric, by the wall.

He too plots a northward journey,
            Virgin of Guadalupe roughly tattooed on his arm.

On this day that smells of citrus and patent leather,
    he moves from *sueño* to nightmare.

2,501 gone plus the ones who will follow.
    Their spirits hover above the mountains of Oaxaca.

The soil here—earth cracked, eroded—has lost its verve.
How reclaim the departed if they can't take root.

    With Zacatecas clay, we map their interiors, trace their travels with
        trembling fingers until a likeness of each one
            rises clairvoyant.

Assembled from fine silt, river water, fired and filled with clamour,
    they summon us with their convulsive beauty.

*

On a long stick, a skeleton capers with its shadow,
while skulls tumble out of the ossuary's crippled doorway.

The concrete is cracked down one side, cacti
                proliferate on the roof.

Because, playing slide guitar, he can seduce any god,
      the mathematician folds his arms inside his soft-collared jacket,
         and refuses Diego's tinted, obtuse-angled portrait.

           In the bare fields, the upright coffin displays a dead girl
with family members in formal attitudes of grief.

Her twin, rebozo tight across her shoulders, closes her eyes, and vanishes.
We cannot master the black dogs.

A stark face and a starfish peer from the Aztec causeway—
         so far from the sea, so near the underworld, thunderstruck.

*

Rojas' musical beings electrify the lobby of the Hotel Nikko,
    brilliantly scored in crimson, achromatic,

   eclipsed by nothing, fearless, roaming the morning corridors,
infiltrating the dreams of the guests, choosing their harmonics: flute,
      tuba, percolator.

*

We experience different versions of the same night.
In this one, we race to the basalt outcrop of Chapultepec

with two variegated maize cobs in one hand and four pebbles in the other.
    In a pond the primitive, grappling fish

fight over a heel of bread as young children
    vigorously stir the algal water, shrieking.

*

    Following Maximilian's execution, his eyes
were replaced by glass eyes borrowed from the Virgin,

        affording him a rare entree into the afterlife. On Saturdays
        thieves circle the Zócalo, the navel of the moon,

    still awaiting President Alemán's promise from the 1940s:
a Cadillac for every Mexican. Or at least a cigar.

        I write from the foot of Popocatépetl
after immersion in Eisenstein's *¡Qué viva México!* Instead of spines,
    this metal cactus is covered with small plastic hands.

*

After a blazing, dramatic death in a plane crash,
    Pedro Infante danced on the tezontle stones of the Plaza Garibaldi.

When queried about his demise, he said
        the shape of his pain was inverted, black persimmon

and pale cedar with a dizzying effect, say antifreeze after hot mustard.

Turbulent Primitive

Triangles foretell an auspicious day for deer,
    circles a looming sandstorm.
        The earth-coloured forked stick says take this path.

Blood-smeared oblong with a carbon dot, Mars ponders war.
    Four clustered sprigs, a spring nearby.
        A pickaxe looms. Here come the grave-robbers.

Nothing is sacred, reality a long way off,
    the hazard hidden in the stone,
        in this unusable portion of desert,

poisoned oasis. Velázquez, deliver us
    from these shadows, paint us back inside time.
        Give us the shrewd, suspicious eyes of Pope Innocent X,

the frenzied, illusory life of Madrid's court.
    Natural illumination is vanishing, each day is a little dimmer.
        Come, on this turbulent afternoon, sit with me

beneath this large chunk of sandstone
    which tilts, wobbles above its smaller base—
        first the clouds are shredded, then the statuary

topples. Mountains crumple. Our every orifice
    is crammed with sand. In the aftermath, the choice
        is clear. In the desert one kills for water.

The Tail of Ted Hughes' Fox

Beneath a dense, fuchsia cloud of unknowing
I can see and almost touch the five stages of women,

a decade apart. Sisters, or distant cousins?
Strange shoes adorn their feet,

they clutch 1950s handbags on the wide road to burning
every brassiere. In their tight-fitting

pillbox hats, they are nearly sightless.
The comet is nowhere in view,

but the salt flats are here to stay, on riverbeds
that uplift and overflow

with briny, undrinkable water. A fox tail whips
back and forth from an ancient aerial, so long species, adieu,

no longer trotting slyly into Ted Hughes' neocortex,
whose skull is encrusted with diamonds and sold

to the lowest bidder.
The permanent is leaving town.

The underworld calls from a seashell I placed
by my ear once in a state of great dismay and agitation,

and it lulled me into a deep, warm, golden sleep,
but I have been rudely awakened and sleep is *verboten*.

I recall dressing in Turkish costume for my ballet troupe,
baggy satin trousers, long-sleeved blouse

and short, snappy vest. Performing, I felt threadbare—I am not
a good dancer—and why we girls wore fezzes—

I thought of mine as a reliquary—was never clear.
I lost one ballet slipper, its elastic strap

hand-stitched by my grandmother, so I left early.
Today I am without provenance, and the rain is on loan.

Self as Parchment

The music of the spheres is iron-hard and brutal.

Obscure bittersweet notes form a prelude, like frosting.

I am dog-eared and decadent.

Layers of paint on the wall ripple like yearning
for the sea. Their motion immobilizes me.

The supernatural enters me while I seek sleep.

Bone by bone, a skinny dappled boy materializes.

I love glacial till. It's all I'll ever experience of farming.

I float in the blue bayou, indolent, saddened, maddened.

A clangy *objet d'art* zings by.

Red-lipped, sugar-coated, in my nightgown, I descend and descend.

Not as Perceived in the Phenomenal World

The night sky hums sea green, infinite, the quarter moon is
     borderline blue.

The triangle, the dissected circle, give way
to oak, apple, elm, hemlock, beech, bathed in stone-washed pink
                          and enigmatic orange.

Onto unruly fields fall the offspring of weeds, the lowly
the pioneering, the unloved.

When gazing up from underground, between the raw
                       tangles of roots,
through pinholes we imagine azure sky,
     pearl cloud.

Out of her depth, a woman grips a large struggling fish
                      under one arm.

Moss wavers, a goldfinch vanishes in the forsythia,
our compass spins.

Here's a belly dancer, a thrill of zills.
Into the sun parade troubadours, irrational musical notes, the letters
                    Q and R,
disappearing Morse code. We yodel
     mouth to mouth at fever pitch.

In the metropolis the wind has ceased.
We're stranded with rings of carbon or Saturn, an excess
                  of free radicals.

Background of Enchantments

Roofs with near-perfect pitch.
Chimneys bob up and down
like player piano keys. A Russian farmer steps out of Tolstoy
and finds the mildewed, wood-framed church

aslant, his hat and potatoes sunk in mud, a parachutist
behind enemy lines, years out of date.

Matchstick stairs lead to a dollhouse kitchen,
a twig bridge from one room to the next.

Slumped in exhaustion, the bust of a man
in jaunty sailor hat digresses frantically from his prepared speech.

*

In night, the wide unblinking eye of a chameleon,
my darling and I float in the unconscious,
motorcade and Jackie in a lamé suit, destined for
a handshake or a goodnight kiss, my appetite, his mouth.

Love is now an interior in flames, a metal jacket.
In lieu of touch there's an earthquake.
In a parking lot, we pitch forward on hands and knees,
landing face to face with a depot of used tires.

Night Deeper than Water

Nothing but a washed-out mandarin edge, a tin of worms
open on the table.

Subatomic particles collide and circulate
languidly as fan blades stir the humid air.

She is trying to squeeze her way into my heart,
that wild turkey bobbing in the yard.

Who arranged those vertical splashes of light
halfway up the sky?

The drifter and I are hanging on
by our teeth. Each morning he asks,

how can we live in the woods,
among the decaying stars?

In his cowboy hat
and laminated T, he runs

from this and that, mutters
strange sayings, won't feed the fish.

The Character of the Accidental

Light beaming from the roses at dangerously delinquent
velocities makes a pact with the subliminally erotic.
                        Why won't I?

In one of her introspective moods our teenage friend wears
cherries hooked over her ears.
Sunning head-first between her breasts,
her irascible pet iguana scares off prospective beaus.

Blurry circles, a.k.a. soap bubbles in
infrared time, are provocatively and distractingly
strewn across the seascape. We suspect
they are harbingers of bizarre, conical thunderheads.

Unexpectedly the cold swells and billows.
We recognize the way forward,
negotiating with ice crystals,
hoping the violent wind
doesn't whirl that unmoored house off to Uranus.

Sheet Metal Music

Moored dreamily and rocking like the elderly
beyond recall, on a whim we leap from beribboned flanks
of forest straight onto the tethered riverboat,
grab fiddle and washboard, mingle
with the ever-changing crew and gamble away the past.

By day three we are ravenous
        and maroon-skinned trees
jitterbug wildly a few metres above the water.

        Rather than steer, the captain takes to his
trumpet. His piercing notes create leaf-fall
and autumn deepens. Frogs hibernate
in enormous heaps and water moccasins sway to his beat,
temporarily relieved of their aggressive souls.

Cedars arch overhead like archaic elements
        in medieval sculpture, the midnight horror tree
with its dentures clattering. We vault over the side.

        Past magnolias ripening and winding their cloying perfume
around and around our breasts, past sweet gum
and cat briar, we glimpse The Door of No Return
in the sun-pocked distance. We mistake it for our exit
and jump through, colliding with somebody's Delta blues.

Years in a Leaky Boat

Out beyond the bleak headland, the horizon buckles.

We veer into primeval red brine, brimming, like
a haemophiliac's ceaseless flow.

Cherry-red sandbar on a dungeon-black field.

Sunburnt, roasted sea.

We envision our sloop as a phantom ship, rigging
frayed, mast in splinters. Aftermath.

We invent a plucky heroine: up at dawn,
determined to break the around-the-globe-solo record.

The dark field of the poem ripples.

This is a quasi-representational work of art—
no to "red sky at night,"
yes to scorpion red beneath the prow.

Into the Void

The Former Danceuse Contemplates
an Eggplant-Tinted Galaxy

Daffodil on a stick, pinwheel or discarded magic wand,
the usual array of exploded stars, a vast indifference.
Her skirt, electric antique lace, froths and bubbles
like Hokusai's surf. In the deep shade of her eccentric hat:
a great stir of electrons, a flicker in the opalescence,
poised to push against some larger circumference.
Fragrance of forgotten choreographies.
Windows silver-streaked and backlit.
She's elusive, then stratified, then transparent.
She fears only the hazards of nightblack.

*

Into pulsating silence she is flung,
uranium-eyed, imprisoned in static electricity, adjusting
for night-blindness. She becomes a horizon, blackouts
emanating from so many paper cuts.
Lava bubbles into her sleep. Subterraneously she inhales
volcanoes. She plots an expedition
to her interior, lit by a rapidly sinking moon.
Crunch of bones and charcoal
underfoot. Tread lightly. Oh Siqueiros! One
gloved fist, raised, calls down fire.

*

She has a tambourine, not an obligation to family.
A dead ringer for no one, she's a slurry of human feeling
travelling through the barren topography, captivated
by its misdeeds. Painstakingly, she lifts her foot.
Romantic suffering is everywhere. There's a scorpion

with stinger raised, constructed of eighteenth-century
Japanese armour, burnished but brooding like a scholar.
In the second take she lowers her foot, kicks sand,
flings away her tambourine. The scorpion
jumps sideways, uncannily levitates.

*

On the ground appears a labyrinth of ink cubes and variations
on indigo. She is loose, at a loss in the semi-dark.
The magnified tenor sax hyperbolic.
The Mickey escapade, did you catch that?
Her fingers elongate into piano keys, flashing ecru,
then iridescent blue. She's searching for separation
of body and mind, while everyone else foments
amalgamation: sticks, straw, memories.
The labyrinth has no heart and the exit
is blocked, so she takes a long detour, through saturation
into virtuosity, and beyond.

The Woman Who Followed the Dotted Lines

Against a backdrop of pale yellow
enthusiasm, ocean song, and an empty nursery,
    longing for vision, for the mystic,
or at least to be released from her coat of mail,
    she's taking flying lessons.

Her eyes are close-set on top of her head—
mesmerizing. The grass beneath her is browning,
    shearing.

    It's nearly noon
and her twin tails shift up and down in a capricious wind.
Obsidian arrow, skyscraper-tall,
by her side. Nothing to register

but the shimmer of event, a sketchy
history of her rubber boots, her leaping
    straight up.

Tomorrow's Bright White Light

To count the eyes of forest creatures,
the stripper goes on an outing.
Frost glitters in the short-cropped fields.
They are not her fields but she claims their souls.
They are not under any sky.
     At rest among the bloodroot, she admires
the only thing in view—her
unencumbered arm, now a queer, cold tone
of green, as though reflecting conifers
and spirits commingled. The other arm, encased
in leather, triggers vivid memories of the
Superior Glove Factory.
She'll die alone,
the residue of a photograph. At her side
is a pile of dusky plums, plundered by wasps.

Close to Ghosts

With a tape measure, the supermodel loiters in a graveyard.
A rock-bottom sensation is what she's got.
One early killing frost has followed another.
Pumpkins glow in the field like planets
of a brand new solar system.
The void that surrounds them seeps inside her head.

When she feels especially dreary she crouches
like a lion on the hunt
behind a fence of peacock feathers.
Except for the workers trimming bushes,
it's very quiet.

The fog shifts, the ghosts stand up
and ask if she's hungry. She nods,
doesn't mention she's on a diet.
The ghosts gather. Long, skinny faces,
even on the fat ones. Her legs
start sinking into the ground.
When the grass reaches her knees, she'll scream.

Vertiginous Sky, Don't Embrace

The wayward daughter heads
for the foundered villa, its walls whitened
to near-blue, curtains drawn halfway to the sky
—a mere diagram of sky
constantly lit by flares.
A hundred windows, some
boarded up, a gangplank protruding
from the topmost. Above that, a rash of stars.

Behind the Japanese panels her mother
is painstakingly pouring scented paint
over a bowl of peaches when the flamenco
dancer arrives. The place fills up,
the evening thrums.

Later, by starlight, some guests race across
the pitted fields, too late discovering ankle-wrenching holes
but put off seeking help until morning.
Cracks in the walls reveal secrets,
as if viewing Bergman on acid
with an overenthusiastic, insistent stranger.
A fenestrated box with an iron grip stands sentry
while a tailgate vanishes, winking out of sight
around the bend that led her, initially
unfettered, to these sere mountains
for a little love, a fractured star.

She can't be cajoled into getting out of bed,
much less to stagger onto the sooty
patio, past overturned urns, lawn chairs,
the trampled remnants of violets. Her mouth twists.
She's in one of her bleak periods and can't see
out the (frosted) window.

Marilyn Monroe: Andy Warhol: Marilyn Monroe

Her platinum-yellow wig, hand-painted,
is woven entirely of dead people's hair.
Please speak up, Miss M, he implores.
She clamps her lips shut,
concealing her ivories, false
from bottom to top.

She prefers champagne but it's vodka
and her little charcoal number, backless and feckless,
that uncork her subconscious.

He knows the exact reach
of her phony mole-near-the-lip-thing,
warm stinking air pulsing up from the
subway, ballooning the chiffon blossom of her skirt.

There's something overpowering about that hair,
how many foot-candles?
Here she is lounging on the counter—
satin doll, temptress—reliving her past,
starring in a peep show inside a cherry tree.

Extreme Condition

After the screw-up, the astronaut invents a reason for each action.
She complicates every incident, even side by side
    with her sweetheart in the glossy,
refurbished brochure kitchen. Dengue Fever,
the Cambodian-American band, revs into überdrive,
then crashes in a blither
        of cellular sonics—her vibrating monocytes
gobble up units of enemy virus. T4s mobilize, humming.

The ever-accumulating lead and zinc jingle percussively.
   But, she intervenes, springing nimbly from her
slick-as-eel-skin, thin-walled Zodiac, *zinc boosts your vitamin C!*
Though lead seepage inhibits formation of the myelin sheath,
        creating havoc, one nerve fibre at a time.

Coming out of orbit, she alights on a wrinkled, pocked vastness
        near a crater overgrown with crystals.
Toss the dross, she insists, *survival of the*—glancing sideways
at her unexpected simian companion, she buttons her lip
and rolls her tongue. Let *it* lick the lead paint
next time the astrobiologist pushes
    their nearly obliterated luck.
This planet a mere lexicon of the one left behind.

How they stomped the night away,
    pantòmiming an inelegant *pas de deux*,
space boots trumping monkey feet. Later, they lingered
over cookie dough and the last *pain au chocolat*,
      butter like they'd never seen it before.

Lost Traveller

A Disturbance in the Key of B

Arms crossed, I lean on the tabletop.
    It's a public place and I'm really hungry
but I hate eating in front of others.
    It's either squish food down in two or three bites
or chew each mouthful one hundred times,
    a feat I've managed only once, on mescaline,
with an apple. A human
    might be watching. If I were invisible,
I would crave to be noticed.
    Art carries no straightforward message,
so it can always mean the opposite.
    When I was in grade school a family friend
exhorted me to be whatever I wanted. If I said explorer,
    he'd wink, but if I said writer, he'd
throw up his hands and leave the house.

    My room has a mahogany door and shuttered
windows. Beyond the veranda,
    the painted concrete emulates lawn.
Even so, I want to lie down on it with a grass stem
    between my teeth.
When I finally force myself to go out the door,
    rather than vault over the window sill,
I've run out of oranges.
    The sky clouds up, the stars are invisible.
It feels like infinity
    could take up residence in me, some rough place
like my liver that won't see daylight.
    Where are the sources of the self? I need to find mine
and give them a good shaking.

En Famille: Latent Body Language

Up to this moment, my life has been horizontal,
spent in a virtual rectangle inside a large cupboard
on its side with its single door quietly, irrevocably
removed.
Three of us—mother, father, daughter—are squeezed in here,
no trinity but a lark of inventiveness.
Wires cradle our heads.
We are patched at the shoulders, inked at the hips.
Camera-shy.

The shelves are covertly lined with butcher paper
and I'm convinced—I read this somewhere—
the shape of my head mimics the worn handle
of a kitchen knife. The whole cupboard
is outlined with handles of knives jammed into the wall.
A fence no one breaches.

The one on the bottom is naked,
squashed and very cross. Pitiful,
nothing but black inside his c-r-a-n-i-u-m.

Wilderness of One

In head-to-toe straitjacket, I stand numbly
in a corner, facing ugly, spit-slick walls.

If you only knew to what lengths I have gone
to make it here, motionless as a straight pin,
in padded cotton booties,

you would wonder what I was doing before:

a) conducting an orchestra?

b) stretched out, sunbathing, in a field of watermelons?

c) ripping the caps off thousands of soda bottles?

d) snugging a lariat around the neck of my father
(for very good reasons)?

I have drawn a schematic picture representing each day of my life.
Many are white or blank. Some are etched by raindrops.
The puddle days are the best, jammed with mysterious
reflected beings and inverted trees.

I wandered back roads on my unicycle, practicing with my lariat.

My father stepped backward, away from me
(I was wearing a ski mask), tripped, fell—
bubbles dribbled from his mouth.

If I stand here long enough I will probably faint.
The attendants are hoping for it.

Omniscience Is Overrated

Beyond description or bereavement,
        my days in the drift zone:

figures from dreams,
    trapezoidal forms on wires,
        minute, artful.

Many lines of energy bend toward a single opening—
    on one side singing, weeping on the other.

        In this force field objects collect:
a traveller's palm, wobbling ladders,
    my brother,
    balanced on a single piano key,
        spotlight blazing on his face.

Exhilarated, he sings off-key, startling birds.

    Through archways, behind beaded,
        tasselled curtains, botanical nurseries
        are revealed.

Earth's crust is alight with mica, feldspar.

        No one builds palaces.

Lovesick

About to pitch forward
into a wavering morass of goldenrod
I hold up one hand—I can work against gravity
though balance might be a long shot.
I come indoors wearing clothes
steeped in the plush hues of summer
and light passes through me.

Peering beyond the deck, I feel sumac invading
from the edge of the forest.
I set up dominos in ordered groupings
representing people I once worked with in an office.
The twos and sixes behave greedily.
I sweep the lot onto the floor.

*

Here is an interior, flat and unreflective,
where we don't need names.
I get down on all fours, the atmosphere crackles
in my electrical field.
At twilight I glimpse my reflection.
I look like someone possessed,
with a misshapen head.

Installation (Venice)

Moon breaking cover, hello to my father
    dead a year
    without whom I am lonely.

Plaintive voice of childhood recalled in archetype
or watercolour, strains of opera
    and *Winnie-the-Pooh*.

*

Today at Ca' Pesaro in the Galleria d'Arte Moderna
I was mesmerized by fractured light
    rippling through old glass

—accidental art, of which my life is constructed.

Each day I see what I can see.

*

Underneath it all, the old inarticulate feelings
    converge, Pegeen Vail commits suicide,

    leaving a trail of primitive paintings
numbered backward to zero, then
irrational numbers *sans* musical tone.

*

Bitter as an onion, sulky, gay, recognized late in life
        by few, Bice Lazzari, dead 25 years,
sits in an old metal chair, brick-red.

        A storm arises but she continues to paint.
        Brush stroke after brush stroke, she keeps on,
the view lost in fog and mist. She sits

        by a wire fence, dabs
a bit here and there by headlamp
                —this after her informal period.

Abruptly, silver and four-sided, lightning
        skids across her canvas.

Reality Beside Itself

I'm strolling across cerulean snow in this intermediate realm,

    animated plants above ground and, below,
a triumph of tubers, roots, vegetative stuffing.

        Giant stick insects trade places among the conifers.

A narcotic wind keeps me from feeling any loss too deeply.

My reflection, trapped in ever-widening gaps between panes,
    is no longer recognizable.

Bare-headed and bare-backed, something pink occurs.

    As a child, I'm jammed into the back seat between two
        slabs of beef. A rodeo taking place nearby.

No water in the aquifer.

    A solitary bee
        zigzags toward a redbud on the hilltop.

My point of view? Harmless and aimless,
    sexual fantasy's "voluptuous" is disappointing in the flesh

    —I'm inconsolable, burying corpses
        with the gravedigger's son.

Here in the east, larkspurs stir and this lost traveller
    finds her way through a hailstorm, having left windows open

in every previous town.

The Future Isn't What It Used to Be

My triangular handmade hat box and I zoom
on a hoverfly toward the limestone building

    with detachable steeple. Fresh snow
    on the ridge cools me down in milliseconds.

There's a caribou-head-with-antlers
paperweight in the corner office.

    Did I say an abbreviated version of a Buddhist chant,
    a single inhalation with the one good lung left

after sandpaper was aggressively applied?
Monsoon, early June, me up to my neck in it.

    A tipsy rectangle settles itself casually down
    as an *haute* chartreuse seamount

erupts on the ocean floor, the ash blending just so
with the decelerating mid-Atlantic current.

    My soul, shrunk to the size of a minnow,
    gasps for water, flops on the scarred river

bank. Open the coal black door
beneath the building's overhang, hold one finger

    under the rusted hot water tap, run for cover.

Earlier in Paris

My face is a natural disaster, a tsunami
swarming toward land with naked red bacteria
in its maw.
I'm invisible at night, tired of talking.
I crouch near my pet rabbit and hum.
Miss Josephine Baker, whom I just met,
squeezes in beside me
as if we were reunited accident victims.
She's overwhelming like a freshly cut papaya,
oozing tropicality, filled with eroded delight.
Can this possibly be the present?
Or just half an hour into the past?
Glamorous, semi-divine, she hides
behind her cashmere scarf.
I believe that's me, hovering above that birch,
sipping air for sustenance.
She wears her trademark perfume, Bending the Narcissus.
I wear my blemishes.
I can hardly wait for nightfall.

The Erotic Error Bar

Throughout one overcast day, symbols appear
on my upper arms. Occult revival, must be.

I take refuge in a minaret.

I'm too busy suppressing my erotic inclination
to evaluate even this close air.

Cuba is burning, sings Ibrahim Ferrer. Perhaps it is
because I wondered if it could. If I could. Set a fire from afar.

I begin a serigraphic monologue about daily life,
boring in large doses. I can't stop.

I want no one else to speak for me.

I spent yesterday kicking a half-empty soda bottle
up and down a mountain.

Most nights I explore neighbourhoods near and far,
gather bundles of plastic and newspaper.

I no longer stay at the bombed-out Ritz:
too many ashes in the swimming pool
and no laundry service.

Titanium and Kryptonite

Nailed to a high stone wall I find a musical score composed
of titanium and kryptonite.
Farther along, an inflammable waterfall and Rapunzel's
kinetic hair.

A star box, a hundred star boxes,
foldable as origami,
        for packing in rocket ships.

My pencil sketch of Klee's head cocked to one side, a tiny hatched
patch—a monocle or galaxy—
a nod to Van Gogh but without immersion of blue
& yellow self in Japanaiserie.

A pilot swings low over an imaginary garden,
a sharp-shinned hawk hustles a snack,
        vole tartare.

The sun is hidden by its second, larger self (as though
predicted by Copernicus).
I prefer the off-balance gyroscope theory; others, the
flawed propeller blade

or engine with asthma attack. A haze
was seen or not, autumn wheat light
        in which to drown.

I advise a focus
on infinite blue
in the event of crash landing. Or the fuselage
already at rest

among corn stalks, intense visionary glow.
Sugar maple borrows branches
            and two crows,

raucously counting.
Meanwhile I superimpose
one horizon onto another. Strewn around are
prehistoric agricultural implements

side by side with plastic artefacts,
one dying culture
            breathing life into another.

Art Exists Only in Relation to Desire

I head out into the luminous morning,
extra clothes in my vinyl bag. Who knows
when I'll return? The sun clinks into its slot,
the Pacific laps at my toes,
undercurrent like a little flame
within the translucent water.
Never mind the violent boys, the Turkish baths,
the movies. The sinewy contours of my body
are foresworn at the end of the boardwalk.
Fires ravage the hills and the sea sizzles.
Above the glassy depths, a dilapidated plane
skywrites lyrics from an Almodóvar film.

*

After dinner I enter a loft in a gritty downtown district,
quickly change into cowboy boots and skimpy,
lacy undergarments. I uncoil a compact whip.
Afterwards, naked, the client exercises
in front of a mirror.
I blot out this segment, pack my bag.
He's handsome in a crude way,
but strip everything away and he's a mere parvenu,
with no formal tradition to fall back on.

Storm-Damaged Alphabet

Beyond billowing curtains on a windswept stage,
    telephone poles lean haplessly, holding
    each other upright like drunks.

I scream and race up rickety stairs.
    In place of the sun—an immense ball of yarn.
    Cardboard wings lowered and bound

to my shoulders, I am speechless. A diamond window
    in the wall scintillates, a postage stamp is raised on a flagpole.
    Waves sweep away the bathers lined up

outside their cabanas, hoping for a tan. To rescue the alphabet
    I climb a ladder. Water hyacinth floats on the roof,
    southern flora are putting down roots.

The signs are unmistakable: delirium,
    but well-intentioned. Seminal brown ink-marks
    blurring in the continuous rain.

I find a pair of stilts. I've never felt so marooned
    between any two points of land.
    I display a forced smile to get help.

In the scramble for a jacket
    I miss the life-boat. Now bobbing up and down
    on the flattened, gas-streaked sea.

Labyrinth

Ruined City

In this year of dread Klee sees
    that the future is farther in, deeper down
than his fingers, hands, arms, will.

Alone in his studio he can't sleep.
    Intricate miniature machines preside,
a bespectacled man in a pear tree

goes blind, flamboyant fruit suspended
    above his grasp. In pursuit of beauty
Klee adjusts style to match cramped fingers.

Stitched together by strands of lacework:
    a mountaintop city, firmament above, fields
below, drenched in burnt sienna.

At the apex of the fortifications, hidden
    behind parallel lines, sun and stars alike
are scorched, sombre, dark—

an end to feeling.
    Even the fields appear barren.
Where will tenderness blossom?

Not among these crooked streets, blasted trees.
    How bereft he feels, climbing
into the walled city, thirsty,

exhausted, now waiting in line for a sip
    of cool water,
hunkered pensively on a wooden crate

overlooking the textured countryside:
        former grapevines, tobacco fields,
the ransacked forest. Night sinks,

spreading downward from the walls.
        His fingers blacken, useless,
numb. The skin tightens around his lips.

In luminous scraps he carries his pictures inside
        then sketches, paints, scrapes,
until one slides away, complete.

The next picture takes its place, its ancestors
        in shadow. He reels, stumbles down
the medieval stairway he painted to ascend.

Now, in the fields, wind flings grit,
        stinging his face and hands, tasteless
and pointless, for miles. Nearby, his sculpture

seems enigmatic, like his latter-day angels.
        He heads for the coast. Nothing
surprises him, not the thought of dying for art

or in the service of music. His fellow travellers,
        silent, head seaward. Flying fish
leap on board. Soon they cover him.

Laughing, he can barely stand.
        Gently, he tosses the fish back,
his skin glistening with scales, rainbows.

Unquantifiable

He isn't himself since.
Lips thinner, chin doubled.
He lives in a large cardboard box under the railway bridge.
He swings along the trestles in the evenings,
sometimes drools, sometimes whistles an old tune
about District Six.
Flecks of memory whirl across his mind
competing with a diorama in which he peers at a train
racing overhead in early summer.
There's been too much rain, a mist hangs.
He recalls backing away from someone who was shouting.
He was pleading with her, then his shirt was in shreds.
Only tufts of his hair were left.
When he rubs the shiny patches of his face and neck
her voice is nearly audible.
To hear better, he bends to ground level
among the centipedes and beetles.

Lacquered Tail and Fins

He's wearing pitch-black, low-slung swim trunks.
Breath sucked in, his ribs can be counted.
His face is the colour of smashed green peas,
his avatar's a drunken mermaid
clinging to a barnacle-studded rock.
He chews the fortunes from Chinese cookies
hoping to absorb the meaning.

How will I conduct my life?

Is torture always completely, absolutely barbaric?

Aren't I erotic (enough)?

The strings that tie his wrists are frayed, easily
snapped, yet they maintain his integrity.
The grey of his hips shows his old-man self,
waiting, watching.
He's unsure if he will exchange his legs for a tail and scales.
Posturing for the photographer makes him vulnerable–

How can I seduce him?

Air swirls around his punctured skin, flickers
at his wrists and ankles. It's nearly pornographic.

Orpheus' Garden

has no end of alabaster fountains,
    jewelled animals with cold mountain water
        spouting from their jewelled mouths.

Touches of Gaudí everywhere, columns of Picasso marble.

Constructing it took, takes, eons.

Before the garden was,
    before Orpheus,
        Eurydice danced delicately here.

*

The entrance is up uneven wooden stairs,
    past a fence of frost and fossil sea shells.

More Japanese than Greek, more linear than contemplative.

The horizon's opaque and pearl-grey,
    unsettling pink where the sun hisses
but neither rises nor sets.

Many handsome lyres hang from the disintegrating pergolas.

He is not exactly present, not exactly absent.
    Eyes closed, water lapping at his knees.

    Luminous musical notes surround him.

Unnoticed, Rilke whispers in his ear.

*

The shadows lengthen. He has moved
  neither forward nor back in centuries.

Rain cools the soil.
    With their wet shining needles
        the cypresses watch like tuxedoed dignitaries.

    He plucks a few notes of a new melody
        then lays down his lyre.
Love is a reflection, an essence.
    It passes. Years pass.

                    *

Rushing on cocaine he misses details:
    the fledgling weeping maple,
        a verdant waterfall beyond the path.

Extreme blue overhead.
            Lithe tree ferns furnish shelter
        from Pythagorean storms.

What we regard as mystic has been exiled.

        One door opens into another, then into the void.

                    *

When Eurydice disappeared, time collapsed.

    The bubbling fountain and the little bells
        she had hung everywhere
            to catch the delicious ocean breeze
        were abruptly silent.

He quenches the fire of music:
digressive, atonal, metaphoric, devotional.

*

The brightness is oddly claustrophobic,
    pressing down Inquisition-like, tarnished, fevered.

        Lightning etches stone, electrocutes the golden fish
        she tended in the sacred pool.

Just when he's thinking nothing could be worse,
    the lanterns explode.
    Sisyphus shows up drunk,
        out of work and mean.

Sunsharp Wave of Event

The whole island is inverted, a bold slab of striated sandstone
or brittle landscape agate, in
a peyote-laced late afternoon swim.

Near its centre is a dazzling egg, a low-slung cloud.

Every last palm is a black palm.

Below the shoreline, a ghostly edifice rises,
awash in ultramarine.

Midnight is never designated, never experienced per se.

In the grim hours of metaphor there are a few fishing boats,
a solitary kayak.

In the matrix: cartilage and bone, hidden pointillist code.

Are we repaired by dreams?

Marine Fauna at Play / After the Sea Quits

Let's put it this way: despite what the cliff-dwelling
art critics decree, in the lower panel
there's a rusty X-and-O-ness,

or a toy locomotive without tracks,

headlight, or conductor.
If the sea bloom is at work,
it's trapped beneath the aura

of those beady fish eyes, on the same side of the head,

so vision-enhancing goggles are a must.
Dive into the remote, frigid depths
in the upper panel

where the flounder progenitor lurks, smirks.

Had enough yet? Proto-orange and binder-twined,
the lost declaration bobs to the surface
and the treaty is waterlogged and shit-faced,

with hundreds of delegates wooing,

cajoling, clandestinely torturing,
until the flounder is criss-crossed with rope burns,
seeing double.

Some blame this on ship worms.

Ventriloquist

The caller's cape is heart-shaped. He waves
a half-fish/half-moon, pink-tailed.

Casting voice and longing out into a vast
northern moor might conjure a Brontë or two.

*

I shall dwell in any of the peaceful squares, like pixels,
lime or mauve, cross-eyed, unhorsed, bewitched.

Or nimbly balanced on a tightrope above a catastrophic sea,
superfluous and in technicolour, singing a catch.

THE LONG MIGRATION

Architecture Boycott Manifesto

Outdoors: the incised and striped fig-tree bole.
Indoors: crumpled tinfoil ceiling,
my rabbitskin shoes noiseless
as I meander over the glimmering floor.

I'm no nearer to Hundertwasser's
Architecture Boycott Manifesto
or Jamaican Maroon spirit-possession language,
though they might appear in my sightlines.

How did the wallpaper become so besotted?

The plastic fourscore-and-twenty-year-old tablecloth
holds no charms, ringed by thimblefuls of light beer.
This was the view out Van Gogh's tall, mysterious

windows at Arles. Crosswise seating on the puckered
velvet cushion offers a sense of dominion
over the immediate surroundings,
vivid as folk paintings on glass, as portholes in a dream cruise.

The air is intermittently garlanded with aromatic leaf-smoke.

If I were where?
Ally, alloy. If the former, we're deeper than friends;
if the latter, she's a direct descendent of Terminator III

and I'm toast. Her singular tastes
force me into an occluded mirror.
My complexion can't stand the strain.

Dog Star Rising

I recognize that skittering sound—iguana toenails
on high-gloss linoleum. Yes,
Customer Service assures me at the counter, we do animism.

If I lapse into the merely descriptive I fail to adequately
address my feelings.

I had hoped at least once to experience a cascade of pearls.

Beneath the stairs live a scorpion and a dog.
Only in a hammock is sleep possible.

No rain for weeks.

*

Daily, to wash the floor tiles, the housekeeper wets a rag,
stands on it barefoot, and shuffles all around the room.

To protect the inhabitants after cleaning,
she stamps simple glyphs waist-high
on the burnt orange walls.

Her ancient rubber slippers resist firestorms.

The Present Is Elusive

I prefer to live in the cracks of events.

Just this morning I might have leapt out of bed
for the last time as a pin-up girl.

With one good eye and one that sees the devil,
my foundation is blurry.

I'm part of the red bilateral. I have animal magnetism training.

I skip alongside a colonnade of phrases,
backlit and tremulous.

I'm stalled between the intuitive and the conceivable,
with only my sleekly futuristic *Poltrona Flô* as a guide.

Here are the boundaries. They are fissured.

Give Me Your Waterweeds

I'm surrounded by diaphanous foliage, the lime-green sea,
and my shattered boat. Lonesome for the ravine of childhood.

Up to our armpits in sand, the wayward coconut palm and I
wave at imagined passersby.

On the beach, a towering driftwood totem assembles,
and vultures solve complex algorithms
at the feet of a piebald horse.

To become more buoyant,
I eat breakfast—duckweed and water hyacinth.

Into the dead of night the errant blue of the river
carries the Milky Way and me, glimmering and wavering.

The Dream Hole

The ghost of a mosquito shares my bed.

I want a bulletproof car, she said to no one
    in particular.

When composed of silk or smoke,
    I can slip through the dream hole.

In my brocade suit I cut a narrow swath
    through Peter Doig's eclectic leitmotifs.

I had a canary from the C— Islands. It imitated
    the sound of wind and waves in Spanish.

What I miss most in jail
    is the purple spangle of my starry nights.

Though my father is reduced to fine ash
    he is effortlessly rekindled in my mind.

I sent a telegram to my frog on the anniversary
    of its metamorphosis.

Condemned to be black, crows barnstorm the lawn,
    the tumbled, lustrous petals of magnolia.

Oystercatcher School

A playful soapstone coffin carved in the essence
of a middle-aged dwarf elephant, and

my proposed attendance at the oystercatcher school
foiled... Can you blame me if I crave the epithet

muscularly architectonic, as applied to Jenny Holzer?
Or Barthes' quadrad: *fascination, emptiness, pain,*

voluptuousness? I think tribalism is too fetish-focused,
so I dip my legs and arms repeatedly in ink to appear

and disappear with night. You will not see my trail.

Retro Avant-Garde

The crocodile contemplates me through a pastel fog of
hexagons, front feet crossed,

back feet on a makeshift royal dais.
His sheepskin jacket is askew. He opens his jaws

and a cone of light emerges like he's swallowed
a subway car.

With difficulty, time jerks a bit forward.
I'm filled with a cold, crushed sensation—

all the lovely precedents have been strip-
mined. What about afterwardness?

The claw and tail prints, up and over the dune,
are no better or worse than a pristine surface.

Hyperbolize this central image, put the brakes on het-up
impulses whirring fast and furious from optic nerve

to some dodgy childhood recollection of snakes,
my illustrated primer on Komodo dragons.

I'd like to break with Aristotelian narrative here
and move onto the adhesive edge

of an image of Mallarmé, editing articles
for *La Dernière Mode* by randomly inserting,

in scarlet, the words *blank, nothingness*. A caprice.
Or read again Mayakovsky's last journal—

to distract an amorous woman on the Moscow-Vladivostok
train, he insisted *I am not a man, but a cloud in trousers.*

Flare (Not an Exit)

A fanatic slivered moon. Flags ripple all over town.

I quiver. Harsh voices of soldiers whirl.

In the bottle-blue evening, terror lurks behind each shuttered blind.

Below me, in the fields, pale dogwood blushes, shakes off rain.

Into the valley creeps a heavy mist. A fox flees.

I arrange my pillow thus: moonrise on the left, moonset to the right.

During the night, beneath my feet, an arcane black accumulates.

Much later I link arms with strangers, cancan out the back door

to scattered applause.

DRUNK MONK

We scooted by another sun-hammered hamlet
    on two or four wheels,

the pre-urban scrawl lodged under
    obfuscated light, unilluminating. Hazy. Teflon.

Jersey Boys. Razor wire deterrents
    as numerous as the yellowed leaflets distributed,

Poisson fashion, from the pugnacious gravel-grown trees.
    Lifespans measured in half-decades,

not half-lives, like before.
    Battened down along the embankment,

tin sheets flex their muscles.
    A voice-over precedes the rustling

of migrant crows. The vagaries of the universe
    are my newest responsibility.

Ether in a hankie pressed hastily against cracked lips,
    I'm required on the train station platform

to plunge a hypodermic into the heart of this guy,
    OD'd and collapsed like Uma Thurman in *Pulp Fiction*.

DRUNK MONK—Meet me at the inbound, your
    firewall or mine.

Teatro Amazonas

The rusted skyline of the port city wavers. In contrast,
     the great southern river emanates a turquoise
   radiant and somnambulant,
and the deep moan of a foghorn from another world is
drowned, fragmentary.

    At the gates of the Chapel of the Miraculous, on bended knee,
an older weeping man, barely conscious and glancing surreptitiously
      at his watch, entreats the glass-enclosed Madonna, while
some class of rodent straight from the imagination of Klee

scrambles across the buckled flooring, and strange benevolent
cacti and euphorbia raise their branches to communicate
   with universal or galactic beings. Growing up
   an atheist I was fascinated by goddesses and gods, angels
simultaneously retreating and warming their hands

over a bonfire. From my hotel window
   I study the opulent tiled dome of the Teatro Amazonas
and what appears to be seaweed rippling across the middle ground.
A spotlit one-eyed man mournfully rings a small dinner bell

and porcupines descend from tropical hardwoods.
The commemorative plate on the wall depicts an English village green
   with pristine houses and lilacs
      rather than hand-painted life cycles of malaria and yellow
      fever. All day against a backdrop of traffic the Solimões

transports dolphins and tambaqui, eels and water lettuce, mosquito larvae,
   my father's ashes, mahogany and rosewood logs.
      Beyond a banana plantation
in the next street is a damselfly-green warehouse where cocaine
can be purchased at gunpoint. Sudden sumptuous peals of bells

from three competing churches, then comets
    and fireworks. In the only Venus flytrap
    in town, a single vermilion beetle
                    divines the future in tea leaves,
while near a window I sit naked and pray for rain.

Kiskadees spiral and twitter—a swirl of chestnut and amber.
Lavender cirrus purpling to indigo, the river slides by,
        the heavens are starless. Kerosene lamps in the *favelas*
    are lit without ceremony.
A flamingo sunset races away from the hazy, perfumed sky. In an

    endless hour the pavement resounds with marching, tapping feet,
the clip-clop of hooves, the echoed zing of streetcar steel.
Sunday mornings horse-drawn carts collect
    used cardboard and metal to fashion into crude shacks—
can poetry change this? In the near dark, the tower of the Chapel

    is floodlit, eerily orange. The rubber barons proclaimed
the Teatro their social club, lighting each other's rum-soaked cigars,
        hawking ceremoniously every few moments
        into personal gold-plated spittoons,
while the rubber-gatherers, chained to trees,

    rendered pale living sap into enormous rubber balls.
Red highlights the low-life, the carved fan
        grows tendrils and roots.
After rain, in the wet glow
all is revealed. Suddenly I see the interior life of each building—

    wires, tubing, pipes, skeletons,
and a painstakingly detailed scale model of the Teatro.
Even its doors and windows open and close, and
the turn of a tiny handle produces a song in the mercurial voice
        of Caruso.

Unabated Minor Miracle

We rearrange objects in a pavilion by starlight.
    Slices of moon, blood orange.

The exposition is complicated by the arrival of a nightingale.
    The Middle Ages, not heaven-sent,

    arrive fourth class, behind an engine
        covered in soot and grime.

Despite migraine, the nightingale attempts to please
    the burgeoning, erratic winds,
    lurid in crepuscular light.

Easy to believe visible reality is merely one isolated phenomenon
    among many, the drops falling faster and harder.

    In the desert we lived for such rain,
with rainflowers urgently bursting into bloom.

    Here, we walk hand in hand, the down-at-heel road
        about to lead us astray

like a bus meandering across the continent, and we're
    wide awake, inside the storm, passing circular trees,

    some sliced neatly in two—a madman's experiment
        with plumb line and saw.

The bus veers west, the storm passes,
    trailing a murky exhaust.

    Night seems endless, the road follows
fallen stars back and forth across a plain.

    Birdsong becomes bird bone, lost melody.

Yellow Moon: Flip Side,
or Cherry Ice Cream, February, Saskatchewan

Early in Saskatoon, in a fog, I wake
from a luscious dream of licking cherry ice cream
in a weathered stone building—might have been

a convent. Out of doors, lacquer of ice
preserves sky as a blued mosaic, chipped
and meteoric. White vacant squares across

Saskatchewan: glimpses of surveyors' ideas
of true north, played out mid-century, mid-
continent, where Joni Mitchell sprouted

and skated and sang in choirs. Glittering, wind-driven,
snow bruises Highway 6, gusty, lusty,
restless, hiding tar perfume.

The last declension of ice forms overhead
and syllables crash, filling cocktail glasses
at the Casino Regina. Airborne, numbered cows

and their auras animate Annemarie's
textured canvases, and an antique clock
is reconstructed upside down,

its innards enhanced by aluminium dragonflies
that spread wings and lift off every hour. So we drove
as far as Buffalo Narrows on a dare. And stayed.

NOTES

Four poems take their titles from phrases in poems by C.D. Wright: "Night Deeper Than Water," "Sheet Metal Music," "Years in a Leaky Boat," and "Give Me Your Waterweeds."

The houses of the inhabitants of paintings of contemporary South African painter Marlene Dumas (1953-), that appear in some poems, have neither front doors nor back doors. Wind blows through them.

Several poems spring from the Bauhaus lectures on art theory, the diary, paintings, and drawings of Swiss/German painter Paul Klee (1879-1940): Genius Genius Genius.

Space Is a Temporal Concept
From household items, Paul Klee made many puppets (perhaps as many as 50) to amuse his son Felix. They had names such as "Step-Grandmother" and "White-haired Eskimo," as well as the two mentioned in the poem.

For Mary di Michele.

Beneath Dishevelled Stars
For Leslie Zeidenweber and Jaime Venguer.

Night Deeper than Water
Peter Doig, *Drifter*, colour etching on Hahnemühle paper, 2001.

Sheet Metal Music
Starting images: *Okahumkee (Some Other People's Blues)*, 1990, oil on canvas, by Peter Doig; and *The Door of No Return,* mixed media, 2001, by Haitian artist Edouard Duval Carrié.

For Faythe Turner.

Years in a Leaky Boat
This poem borrows reds from Peter Doig's painting Baked, 1990, oil on canvas.

The Former Danceuse Contemplates an Eggplant-Tinted Galaxy
Initiated by images in four paintings by Mexican-American artist Leslie Zeidenweber, all dated 2006-2007: *La Bohemia*, enamel on canvas; *Méxcio en negro*, oil on canvas; *Maya*, oil on canvas, and *Mickey*, oil on canvas.

The Woman Who Followed the Dotted Lines
Inspired by a painting by Los Angeles-based painter Doris La Frenais.

For Doris and Ian La Frenais.

Extreme Condition
Dengue Fever: Los Angeles-based Cambodian-American rock band,
formed in 2001.

Installation (Venice)
Pegeen Vail was the daughter of the art collector Peggy Guggenheim and
Dada sculptor and writer Lawrence Vail. In a small side room at the museum,
Galleria Internazionale d'Arte Moderna, on the Grand Canal in Venice,
where the Peggy Guggenheim Collection is housed, are 14 paintings by
Pegeen, who committed suicide in 1967.

Earlier in Paris
Josephine Baker (1906-1975): striking American-French singer, dancer and
actress in Paris.

The Erotic Error Bar
Ibrahim Ferrer (1927-2005) was a world-class Cuban singer and musician.
The soda bottle image is from a video, *Caracoles*, 1999, by Belgian artist
Francis Alÿs.

Unquantifiable
District Six is a residential sector of Capetown in South Africa with an
infamous apartheid-era history.

Orpheus' Garden
For Tony James

Sunsharp Wave of Event
Bomb Island, 1991, oil on canvas, by Peter Doig kept recurring in dreams until
I wrote this poem.

Marine Fauna at Play / After the Sea Quits
Initial image: *Flores Marinas*, s/f, mixed media on canvas, by Oaxacan
(Mexican) painter Francisco Toledo.

For Ross Fraser and Richard Summerbell.

Architecture Boycott Manifesto
Austrian painter and architect, Hundertwasser (1928-2000) developed rather unusual, organic ideas of contemporary architecture. Jamaican Maroon spirit-possession language is ritualistic, spoken during possession by ancestral spirits.

For Larry Sherman

Dog Star Rising
For Marinete Póvoa.

The Present Is Elusive
Poltrona Flô is the name of a flowing futuristic purple chair designed by Brazilian Renata Moura. http://www.renatamoura.com/

Give Me Your Waterweeds
Peter Doig, *Grand Rivière*, oil on canvas, 2001-2002.

The Dream Hole
For L.E.M.

Retro Avant-Garde
The painting that sparked the poem was *Lagarto*, 1997, mixed media on amate paper, by Francisco Toledo. Amate paper is made from fibre/bark, often of the fig *(Ficus)* tree.

Drunk Monk
Pulp Fiction, 1994, directed by Quentin Tarantino.

Teatro Amazonas
For Marcelo Jacobs-Lorena.

***Yellow Moon*: Flip Side, or Cherry Ice Cream, February, Saskatchewan**
The yellow moon in the title is from singer-songwriter Neil Young's *Helpless*. Cameo appearance of cows is from *Much Perspective (Cows are Female Series)*, 2003, mixed media on canvas (woven), by Annemarie Buchmann-Gerber of Saskatoon, Saskatchewan. The clock sculpture is *Time Flower*, 2010, aluminium, bronze, steel wire, sound clock movement, by Jesse Goddard of Regina, Saskatchewan.

ACKNOWLEDGMENTS

Early drafts of several poems were first published as noted below. I am very grateful for the support of the editors of all these literary magazines and journals, in print and online.

The Antigonish Review: "Teatro Amazonas," "Installation (Venice)" (as "Installation One (Venice)"), "Omniscience Is Overrated" (as "Drift Zone"), "Architecture Boycott Manifesto," "Self as Parchment" (as "Red-Lipped, Sugar-Coated")

Arc Literary Magazine: "Give Me Your Waterweeds," "Night Deeper than Water," "Flare (Not an Exit)" (as "Flare")

Barrow Street: "Ruined City"

The Best Canadian Poetry 2009 (ed. A.F. Moritz): "Space Is a Temporal Concept"

The Best Canadian Poetry 2011 (ed. Priscila Uppal): "A Disturbance in the Key of B" (as "Sources of the Self")

www.blueskiespoetry.ca: "Turbulent Primitive" (as "Primitive")

Canadian Literature: "Storm-Damaged Alphabet"

Contemporary Verse 2: "Ventriloquist," "The Woman Who Followed the Dotted Lines" (as "Flying Lessons"), "DRUNK MONK"

The Fiddlehead: "Titanium and Kryptonite," "Years in a Leaky Boat," "Sheet Metal Music" (as "Listen to Sheet Metal Music")

filling Station: "Dog Star Rising" (as "Animism"), "The Present Is Elusive," "The Tail of Ted Hughes' Fox" (as "Cloud of Unknowing"), "Sunsharp Wave of Event" (as "Midnight Is Never Designated"), "Earlier in Paris" (as "Josephine")

The Literary Review of Canada: "Space Is a Temporal Concept," "Unquantifiable"

The Malahat Review: "Not as Perceived in the Phenomenal World" (as "Not As It Is Perceived in the Temporal World")

Pith & Wry (ed. S. McMaster): "Background of Enchantments," "The Character of the Accidental," "Unabated Minor Miracle" (as "Arrival of the Nightingale")

PRISM international: "A Disturbance in the Key of B" (as "The Sources of the Self"), "Lacquered Tail and Fins" (as "Swim Trunks"), "The Erotic Error Bar" (as "Hiding the Erotic Inclination"), "Tomorrow's Bright White Light" (as "Bloodroot")

Regreen: New Canadian Ecological Poetry (eds. M. Anand, A. Dickinson): "The Future Isn't What It Used to Be" (as "Monsoon, Early June"), "Reality Beside Itself" (as "Animated Plants")

Riddle Fence: "Vertiginous Sky, Don't Embrace"

the Society: "Dream Hole," "Close to Ghosts"

Spoon River Poetry Review: "Oystercatcher School"

www.SugarMule.com: "Background of Enchantments," "The Character of the Accidental," "The Former Danceuse Contemplates an Eggplant-Tinted Galaxy," "Unabated Minor Miracle" (as "Arrival of the Nightingale")

"The Former Danceuse Contemplates an Eggplant-Tinted Galaxy," part of the sequence, "Tangerine and Sunflower," was short-listed for the 2008 CBC Literary Awards. "Orpheus' Garden" was a finalist for the Winston Collins Prize, 2009. "Oystercatcher School" and "Marine Fauna at Play/After the Sea Quits" (as "Sea Bloom at Work") were shortlisted for the Arc Poetry Magazine 2010 Poem of the Year Contest. "Titanium and Kryptonite" was featured on the *Fiddlehead* website for the autumn 2010 issue, no. 245.

My greatest thanks to Stan Dragland for his wonderful sense of words at play, who pushed hard when I asked, and helped tease out and articulate a narrative thread that was deeply hidden (from me at least). Special thanks for the March Hare nights, the sweet hospitality and events at Bond Street, the striated stones from the cove, and the introduction to the paintings of Michael Pittman. My husband Carl is my first reader and I am deeply grateful for his insights and edits, always. I would do almost anything Kitty Lewis asked. I'm grateful to Alayna Munce for such careful editing, detailed queries, and for coming to hear me read at the Eden Mills Literary Festival in 2010. That was a special pleasure for me. I thank artist and photogapher Stacy Greene (www.stacygreene.com) for the author photograph that was the outcome of a delightful afteroon shoot in Manhattan. Suzanne Hicks (please visit msuzannehicks.com) graciously provided the colour palette from the wall of her Albany, New York studio and Cheryl Dipede transformed it into a striking cover. I am in awe of the artistic skills of Suzanne and fine graphic design sense that Cheryl brought into play here. Warmest thanks to both.

Jan Conn was brought up in Asbestos, Quebec. She now lives in Great Barrington, Massachusetts and works as a professor of Biomedical Sciences whose research is focused on mosquitoes, their evolution and ecology. She has published seven previous books of poetry.